MW00623158

www.BramcostPublications.com

ISBN 10: 1-934268-80-1
ISBN 13: 978-1-934268-80-3

Bramcost
Publications

Making a Dress in An Hour

By MARY BROOKS PICKEN

Director of Instruction
Woman's Institute of Domestic Arts & Sciences
Scranton, Pa.

A SMART, up-to-the-minute dress cut out, completely made, all ready to put on within an hour! You may receive a 'phone call at one o'clock inviting you to a little impromptu gathering of friends at three, and you can go, if you wish, wearing a dainty new frock made in the time you would ordinarily spend wondering what to wear.

Such is the delight you can find in making your own clothes now that it is easily possible to make an attractive, becoming dress in an hour.

And you can have as many "One Hour Dresses" as your heart desires—in infinite variety, for the "One Hour Dress" is not a *style* of dress, it is a *method of making*. It is a new and simple *plan* by which the dress you select from the many designs in this book can actually be cut out, put together, finished all complete in sixty minutes. And you can create other "One Hour Dresses" for yourself, because different combinations of colors and materials, different finishes and touches of decoration will enable you to have just the dress that appeals to your taste and have it quickly and at little cost.

Remember that to make a dress quickly you must first understand just what you are going to do—then do this step by step in a systematic way. So read the instructions carefully, observe the pictures and note their meaning. First be sure you understand—then go ahead and you can make the dress of your choice with surprising ease.

The One-Piece
One Hour Dress

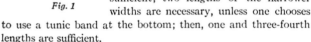

To follow the mode is delightful when it can be done so easily and economically as in the One Hour Dress.

The following pages tell you how to make up lovely silk or wool fabrics into beautiful frocks that are designed and cut without patterns—frocks that express the smartest lines and the newest trimmings in the very happiest way.

Dressmaking is difficult only when you hesitate because of lack of knowledge. Here we have explained every detail so that even though you do not sew, you should be able to make an attractive, creditable dress. And if you do sew, these instructions will be invaluable to you. Fig. 1 shows a smart, one-piece dress made of one of the new striped flannels. Variations are shown on Page 6.

Materials Required.—The 54-inch wool fabrics, such as flannel, wool crêpe, fine Poiret, or charmeen, cut to best advantage in this dress, though the 32-, 36-, or 40-inch material is satisfactory also. One length plus ¼ yard of the 54-inch material is sufficient; two lengths of the narrower widths are necessary, unless one chooses to use a tunic band at the bottom; then, one and three-fourth lengths are sufficient.

Fig. 1

If 40-inch silk is used, a luxuriously long scarf may be made of the strip that is cut from the side.

Taking Your Measurements

Four measurements are required, and these are taken as shown in Fig. 2.

For your *blouse length*, put a pin in the dress you have on a little below your normal waist line or in line with the hip bones, to mark the waist line for the dress you are to make. If you are rather short, this is usually 2 inches below your normal waist line; if medium height, 3 inches; if tall, 4 inches. Measure from the pin in front, over the shoulder, and down the back to a point opposite the pin.

To obtain your *skirt length*, drop the end of the tape measure about 1 inch below the skirt length you want and measure from there to the pin. The extra inch will be taken up in the dart and the fitting at the waist line.

For your *hip measure*, measure around the hips at the fullest part.

For your *armhole measure*, measure around your arm at the shoulder, holding the tape moderately tight.

Fig. 2

Preparing the Material

After taking the measurements and before cutting the material, straighten the edges by cutting or tearing. If wool is used, tear or cut the material straight at both ends before shrinking it, and, if necessary to make it perfectly straight, pull it from the corners on the bias. All fabrics are woven straight, but in the folding they sometimes become crooked. Printed fabrics with large designs are the only kind that cannot be made satisfactory for cutting by tearing or cutting on a crosswise thread. These should be cut with regard to the design.

Cutting the Dress From 54-Inch Material

Folding the Material.—First, lay out the material folded wrong side out through the center lengthwise, selvage edges toward you, as in Fig. 3, and pin along the fold. Measure half the distance from the lengthwise fold to the selvage and put a pin, as at *a*, through both thicknesses. Turn the top selvage up over the fold *b*, with the selvage itself extending beyond this fold. Turn over the folded material so that the other half is on top and bring the selvage edge down to meet the other selvage. Smooth the material out carefully and pin through both folds the full length of the piece, when the folded material will appear as in Fig. 4. This places the material so that the upper part, or fold, makes the front of the dress and the under part, or fold, the back, and brings the one seam on the left side.

Cutting the Neck Opening.—Next, locate the shoulder point at the neck by measuring down, or toward you, 2 inches from *c* at one end of the upper fold and marking *d*. Measure to the left on the upper fold 5 inches from *c* and locate *e*. Then cut on a straight thread from *c* to *e* to obtain the front-neck opening.

Shaping the Shoulders.—Now, to shape the shoulders, measure, for most figures, on the selvage to the left of the corner, or *f*, 4½ inches, and locate *g*. Very square shoulders require 2½ to 3 inches. Sloping shoulders require 4½ to 5½ inches. Then cut through the four thicknesses from *g* to *d* to make the shoulder line. A good plan is first to draw a chalk line along a ruler from *g* to *d* and then cut on this line to insure accuracy. Next, mark the width of the sleeves by measuring to the left from *g* one-half the arm-hole measure and placing a pin, as at *h*.

Cutting the Waist-Line Dart and Under Arm.—Now measure down from the shoulder line one-half the blouse length and over from the fold one-fourth the hip measure, plus 1½ inches, and locate *i*. Cut on a straight grain from the selvage

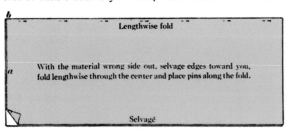

Lengthwise fold

With the material wrong side out, selvage edges toward you, fold lengthwise through the center and place pins along the fold.

Selvage

Fig. 3

Center-back fold   Center-front fold

Fold the material so that the center front and center back come on a fold and so that there will be just one seam at the left side.

Selvage

Fig. 4

edge in to *i* through all thicknesses. This gives the waist-line dart and provides for the plait.

Prepare the under arm by measuring straight to the right of *i* 8 or 10 inches and locating *j*. Then cut in a curved line from *h* to *j*, and straight down from *j* to *i*.

Completing the Cutting.—Complete the cutting of the dress by removing the selvage from line *g h* and by slashing the fold on the under sleeve, doing this so that both sleeves are of the same length.

Stitch left shoulder seam from point 4½ inches from neck edge to armhole.

Fig. 5

The neck is not shaped at this time, as it is advisable first to fit the collar at the neck and then to cut the surplus material away.

Making the Dress

Sewing Up the Seams.—Prepare to sew up the dress, which has five seams. Begin the right-shoulder seam at the neck edge and stitch out to the armhole, using a ⅜-inch seam. Begin the left-shoulder seam, as shown at *a*, Fig. 5, 4 inches down from the neck edge to allow for the opening. Stitch the curved under-arm seams, beginning at the edge of the sleeve and stitching around the curve and down to the waist-line dart. In doing this, keep the edges together accurately by means of pins or baste

Fig. 6

carefully so that the material will not slip.

Next, stitch the side seam of the skirt part, beginning at the waist-line dart and stitching down. When the seams are all stitched, clip the selvage edges every 6 to 12 inches to prevent their drawing; then clip the under-arm seams at the curve, as in Fig. 6, making about five clips in the turn, about 1 inch apart.

Pin the skirt plaits in place, allowing each to come toward the front or back, as you prefer, but with the outside edge of each in direct line with the under-arm seam.

Finishing the Neck Opening.—Finish the neck opening with stay tape or ribbon, as shown in Fig. 7, view (*a*) showing the right side and view (*b*), the wrong side. First clip the shoulder seam, as at *a*, view (*b*), so that the seam will lie flat, and then face the front edge with the tape or ribbon and bind the back edge. Make sure that the back-shoulder binding is as long as the front facing and take narrow seams so that the shoulder seam will not pull up.

(a)

(b)

Fig. 7

Fig. 8

Fig. 9

Putting in the Hip Dart and Side Plaits. Pin in the dart, taking up $\frac{3}{4}$ inch of the material at the seam for the average figure and tapering it to nothing about 2 to $2\frac{1}{2}$ inches on each side. On the wrong side, the dart will appear as in Fig. 8. Pin the hem up the amount allowed, turning an even line all the way around. The skirt length for this type of dress is determined by the hip dart, all fitting being done there. So turn the hem the amount allowed, evenly all the way, usually 3 to 4 inches.

At this time, it is advisable to slip the dress on to make sure that the darts are pinned to give an even line at the bottom, also that the hem is turned so as to make the skirt the correct length.

Pinch the side plaits in, as in Fig. 9, along both sides of the dart to get the effect desired. These plaits really fit the dress to the figure, controlling the fulness enough to make a belt unnecessary. However, one may be used across the back or front or all the way around, if desired.

Remove the dress, stitch the dart carefully, taking up just what was pinned in; then press the dart down, when from the wrong side it will appear as in Fig. 10. Turn the dress right side out, stitch the pinched plaits down, stitching $\frac{1}{4}$ inch from the edge and about 2 inches above the dart and 1 inch below.

Turn the dress wrong side out and prepare to stay the edge of the plait to the dart. First smooth the dress so that the plait will lie flat and on the straight of the material. Then take a few secure stitches, as at *a*, Fig. 10, to hold it firmly in position.

Finishing the Sleeves, Hem, and Neck.—Finish the lower part of the sleeves by using seam tape or ribbon. To do this, apply the tape to the right side and stitch $\frac{1}{4}$ inch from the sleeve edge. Turn to the wrong side, when the stitching line will appear as *a*, Fig. 11; then press down and slip-stitch or stitch in place, as at *b*.

To make a good hem finish, apply seam tape or ribbon on the top of the hem in the

Fig. 10

Fig. 11

Fig. 12

same manner as for the sleeves. Then put the hem in with slip-stitches, taking up as little of the material of the dress as possible but making a secure stitch in the tape, as shown in Fig. 12.

When fitting the dress, try on the collar that you choose to wear with it. Mark and cut the neck line that it requires, allowing for seams. Make sure that both sides of the neck are trimmed the same. Face the neck with a bias strip of silk or other suitable material. Sew two snap fasteners on the shoulder closing.

Fold Lengthwise

Stitch with ¼-inch seam

(a)

Turn belt right side out

(b)

Fig. 13

Making the Waist-Line Finish.—If a belt of the material is desired across the back, seam a 2-inch lengthwise strip together, using the pieces cut from the under-arm for this. Stitch the folded material the full length, about ¼ inch from the torn edge, and across one end, as in Fig. 13 (a). Turn the belt right side out. An easy way to do this is to place the blunt end of a pencil against the end seam and pull the belt down over the pencil, as in (b), until it is turned right side out. Then slip out the pencil. Press the belt and stitch across the open end.

If buckles are used, finish as shown in Fig. 1; otherwise, slip the ends of the belt strip underneath the front pinched-in plaits and secure them in place by means of ornamental buttons, tacking stitches, or machine stitching.

Complete the dress by pressing it and adding the collar and cuffs.

Cutting and Applying Long Sleeves

If long sleeves are desired, fold in the center, lengthwise, a piece of material as long as you want the sleeve and as wide as the armhole measure, as in Fig. 14. Measure down on the lengthwise edges 1½ inches, locating point *a*, and then draw a diagonal line from *a* to the end of the fold, *b*. This gives a pointed sleeve that will fit perfectly into the straight armhole, as shown in Fig. 15.

Baste the sleeve in the armhole and stitch in before the under-arm seams are stitched, as shown. Start at the shoulder seam, as at *a*, to baste and stitch so as to bring the point in exact position and avoid stretching either the sleeve or the material.

Fig. 14

Fig. 15

Fig. 16

For long sleeves of this type, an effective wrist finish is shown in Fig. 16. Fit the sleeve at the wrist with pinched-in plaits and make a turn-over, center-stitched binding at the lower edge, as shown in Figs. 8 and 9, page 14.

One of the lovely new Kasha-like bordered woolens in green and tan with a touch of orange develops the simple and effective model at the left below.

Natural Kasha with orange and navy polka-dotted scarf tie is the ideal choice for the model just to the right, though any neutral-colored flannel may be used.

At the center below is a practical dress of pinky-beige flat crêpe, which is attractive enough for informal wear also. The drape is its distinctive feature.

Tailored collar, cuffs, and jabot of white piqué add to the charm of the pastel striped flannel dress at the right below.

The model above requires 1¾ yards of bordered material. Cut ⅛ yard from one end for the narrow scarf collar. Fold the remaining material crosswise through the center, so that the crosswise threads run up and down. Follow the instruction, proceeding as though the two cut ends were selvages and the selvages were cut ends.

For the model at the center above, follow the instruction, cutting down to within about 15 inches of the bottom of the skirt before allowing for the plait. The small sketch at the lower left shows the wrong side of the plait finish.

Provide 13 inches more than two dress lengths of 40-inch silk for the dress with the front drape. Tear off 13 inches along the end and up the side so that you have a corner for the drape as shown in the small sketch. Cut the dress without allowance for the deep hip plait, and with two selvage edges together in place of the fold.

The striped flannel dress is cut exactly according to the detailed instruction.

Fig. 17   Fig. 18   Fig. 19

Slenderizing One-Piece Dress

If the figure is larger than 40-inch bust and it is desired to use 54-inch material, buy one length plus ½ yard, and use ¼ yard to put a crosswise panel in the center front of the dress, as shown in Fig. 17.   This panel may be stitched in crosswise tuck effect and used as a feature for a slenderizing dress.   Or, if the hips are small in proportion to the bust, the panel may be omitted and a plain seam used and this covered with braid, as in Fig. 18.   The seam may come at the center front or left-side front or right-side back.   In any event, the panel or plain seam should be made complete before the dress is cut out.

Cutting Out the Dress.—Place the material, which is now in the form of a tube, lengthwise, so that the center of the panel makes one fold and this fold is toward you.   Then fold the material in half lengthwise, turning the panel fold up, or away from you, when it will be in the position shown in Fig. 4, with the exception that there will be a fold where the selvages are shown, as this dress has no side seam.   Then cut the dress out as explained and shown in Fig. 4.   When the dress is cut and opened out, the upper part will appear as in Fig. 19.

Shoulder-Seam Dart.—If the bust is slightly full, and ease across the front is desired, or if plaids or checks are to be matched at the shoulder seam, a dart may be placed 1½ inches from the neck curve on each shoulder, as shown in Fig. 17. This may be pressed in ¾ inch deep (1½ inches altogether), and caught just at the shoulder seam, or it may be stitched down, dart fashion, for 2 or 3 inches.   If such a dart is used, it will be necessary to trim off the back section of the sleeve so as to make the sleeve even around the bottom.

Fig. 20

Fig. 21

Applying the Hip Plait and Belt Straps.—The plait at the side over the hips should be pressed back to form an inverted plait, thus making a box plait on the wrong side, as shown in Fig. 20, and an inverted plait on the right.   Catch the box plait securely to the underarm seam with overcasting-stitches, as shown.

To hold the belt in position, wee belt straps are secured in place from the right side just about the inverted box plait, as shown in Fig. 21.   Cut these 1¾ inches wide and 2 inches long, overcast the raw edges together, and press the straps carefully.   Then tuck the ends under, pin the straps in place, as shown, and apply them to the dress by means of invisible stitches.

Cutting the Dress From 40-Inch Material

Fig. 22

The following method of cutting straight-line dresses from 40-inch material is best adapted to figures of from 32- to 36-inch bust measure. It is not recommended to be used for figures larger than 40-inch bust measure. For a 38 figure, take off a 10-inch strip of material where the instruction below suggests removing 13 inches. Then fold the material through the center and proceed exactly as directed.

Amount of Material.—Two lengths, measuring from the shoulder to the bottom of the skirt, are required for the straight-line dress of the season, but less is needed if a band is used at the bottom, as in Fig. 22. Determine the width desired at the point where the band joins the skirt, for example, 54 inches. Subtract half of this width, 27 inches, from 40 inches. The amount left, 13 inches in this case, will be the width of the band. Since this amount is to be added to both the back and the front of the dress, two times 13 inches, or 26 inches less than two dress lengths may be purchased. This is usually $2\frac{3}{8}$ yards of material. If long sleeves are to be added, allow about $\frac{1}{4}$ yard more of material for a dress planned with a band at the bottom, unless plaited sleeves of sheer contrasting material are to be used, when $1\frac{1}{8}$ yards is needed, since each sleeve requires one full width of the material. Two full lengths will provide enough for the sleeves.

Cutting.—Fig. 23 shows very clearly the method of cutting. Cut the 13-inch-wide strip from one selvage of the 40-inch material to be used in one of the ways suggested later. Double the remaining material lengthwise and lay it on the table with the fold away from you. Locate the center point on the fold, as at *a*. Measure down from *a* 2 inches and locate *b*. To the right of *a* 1 inch, locate *c*, and to the left 6 inches, locate *d*. Cut straight from *d* to *b*, and from *c* to *b* with a slight curve. This V-shaped neck may be used with or without a collar.

Straight across the width of the material from *a*, locate *e*; $4\frac{1}{2}$ inches to the right and left of this, locate points *f* and *g*, respectively. To shape the shoulder, cut straight from each of these points to *b*.

To cut the bateau neck line shown in Fig. 22, locate point *h* $4\frac{1}{2}$ inches from *a* in Fig. 23, and point *i* 4 inches to the left of *a*. Cut in a gradual curve from *i* to *h* and from *c* to *h*. Dotted lines indicate these curves, and *hg* and *hf*, the shoulder lines.

Preparatory to cutting the under-arm line, locate *j* on the fold at the hip line of the dress front. From *j*, measure straight across a distance equal to one-fourth of the hip measure plus $1\frac{1}{2}$ inches and locate *k*; 10 inches to the right of *k* locate *l*. Locate *m* at the extreme lower left, and *n* 7 inches to the left of *g*. Cut straight from *m* to *l*; then curve the under arm smoothly to *n*. Use the front under-arm line as a guide in cutting the back.

In order to have the dress hang correctly, the front must be treated in one of two ways, both of which are indicated on the diagram. If the material is plain or of a figure that does not follow the grain closely, the lower edge may be shaped by measuring 1 inch to the right of *m* and cutting in a gradual curve about 8 inches

Fig. 23

toward the fold, as indicated by the dotted line *op*. If the material is striped or corded, raise it by taking in 1 inch in a dart at the hip in the front only, as shown by the dotted lines. Such a dart is usually 4 or 4½ inches long.

From the 13-inch strip that was removed in the beginning, cut the band for the bottom of the dress, making it at least 6 inches longer than the width of the dress at the bottom. This extra allowance forms a plait at the left side. It is necessary to face the band in order to have it 13 inches deep.

From the remaining piece of the 13-inch strip, long sleeves may be cut if an extra ¼ yard was allowed as suggested. These are cut and applied as explained on page 5 and shown in Figs. 14 and 15.

If it is not desired to have long sleeves nor a band at the bottom of the skirt, the 13-inch strip may be used for a scarf, little apron tiers, shirred-on panels over the side seams, ruffles, jabots, or any other similar feature.

The jabot featured in Fig. 22 is made of a straight piece of Georgette or crêpe de Chine, cut 15 inches wide and 18 inches long. Fig. 24 illustrates a simple method of shaping this section. Cut on a diagonal line that will divide the 15-inch sides into 5-inch and 10-inch lengths. Then turn over one of the two sections thus produced so that the two 10-inch widths are at the top and the two 5-inch widths are at the bottom, and the diagonal cut edges are together. Finish the three straight edges of each piece with center-stitched binding, and sew the bias edges to the center front of the dress, covering the stitching with ribbon, as shown.

Making the Dress

Make plain overcasted seams on the shoulders and under the arms. Join the ends of the lower band with a plain seam. Let this seam come in the inside fold of the deep plait that is arranged at the left side, as at *a*, Fig. 25, which shows the wrong side.

Hem or face the band, as at *b*, before applying it. The plait is held only by the stitching that joins the band to the dress, as at *c*. The exposed edge of the plait appears as a continuation of the under-arm seam line *d*.

Make and apply the jabot as described above. Finish the neck and sleeves with center-stitched binding, catching the top of the jabot under the binding.

Fig. 24

Fig. 25

Buttercup-yellow crêpe de Chine makes the dress at the left with its front tucks. The belt and tie are of black or brown.

The shiny side of crêpe satin makes the foundation dress at the right. The black lace becomes an apron or a cape at will.

Sistine-blue crêpe satin suggests soft draping, such as is effected in the model below with its long scarf and front tie-belt.

One of the lovely new bordered crêpes in green and white is used with matching plain green crêpe for the model at the right. The plain band gives a tunic effect that is very smart.

Allow 4 inches for tucks in the front of the model at the left. The small sketch shows how the back of a side seam looks with dart and tucks. Make allowance for a 2½- or 3-inch plait extending from the top of the upper tuck to the bottom of the skirt in one of the side seams. If the belt is of self-material, join the ends in the under-arm seams. If it is of leather, let it slip through openings in these seams.

Cut off a 2½-inch strip from one selvage and use it for the tie-belt on the lace apron of the model above. The dress is cut according to detailed **instr**uction. A side plait may be arranged in the left seam if desired.

Use the long 13-inch strip of material for the scarf and belt of the model at the left. Make the dress according to the detailed instruction. Sew one end of one of the belt pieces in each side seam and tie the belt in front.

Use the lengthwise grain of the bordered material around the figure for the model at the right, 1½ yards being sufficient. There is a deep plait on the left side of the plain green band.

The Two-Piece
One Hour Dress

The type of One Hour Dress shown in Fig. 1, when attractively made of smart new material, is a joy to own. The fact that it is a little less tailored than the one-piece dress makes it more adaptable to a variety of fabrics, from wool to calico, from Swiss to chiffon; in fact, any fabric that does not have a definite nap, such as flat-pile velvet, broadcloth, or similar materials, can be used. Stripes are very smart for it, used lengthwise in the blouse and around in the skirt. Heavy silk crêpes and wash fabrics are ideal.

Measurements and Width of Materials

Take the measurements exactly the same as for the One-Piece One Hour Dress. See Page 1.

If you are more than a 38-inch bust, use 40-inch material. If you are less than 38, 36-inch material is satisfactory. And if you are less than 34, 32-inch material may be used. From 3 to 3½ yards of 36- or 40-inch material are required.

Fig. 1

If you are tall and slender, the only waste in cutting the dress will be that cut out in shaping the neck.

This type of dress is desirable for children, too. The measurements are taken in the same way as for an adult and the dress cut the same except that the neck is made smaller and a 4-inch opening made at the center back to allow the dress to slip over the head.

Dividing the Material

You now divide your material into two parts, one for the blouse and one for the skirt, as in Fig. 2.

Measure off from one end the *blouse length*, and place a pin in the edge of the material to mark the point. Clip through the selvage and cut or tear across. The shorter part is for the blouse; the longer part, for the skirt.

NOTE.—Some materials tear satisfactorily; others do not. The best way to make a crosswise division of material which does tear well is to clip through the selvage edge and tear across. If you prefer to cut it, draw a crosswise thread and cut on the drawn thread line. Materials that pull when torn or that are printed or shaped unevenly on the bolt are more satisfactorily divided by cutting.

Fig. 2

Fold lengthwise and crease here

BLOUSE

Fold crosswise and crease here

Selvage

Fig. 3

Cutting Out the Blouse

Cutting the Armhole and Under Arm.
Fold the shorter piece of material, or the blouse length, first lengthwise, selvage edges together, and then crosswise, as in Fig. 3. Bring one crosswise end up 1 inch to make the front longer than the back and allow for fulness over the bust. Measure to the left from the crosswise fold *a* along the selvage one-half the arm-hole measure and place a pin, as at *b*. Measure from the fold *c* one-fourth the hip measure plus 1½ inches and place a pin, as at *d*.

To obtain the armhole curve, measure straight to the right of *d* 8 or 10 inches and place a pin, as at *e*.

Next, cut straight in from *b*, turning as the pin at *e* is approached and making a smooth, even under-arm curve. Then continue to cut straight down from *e* to *d*, as shown by the dotted line.

Shaping the Waist Line and Sleeves.—To shape the waist line of the blouse, measure up from the bottom ½ to ⅝ inch and place a pin, as at *f*. On the upper piece, which is for the back, taper a curved line from *f* to a point halfway between the under arm and the lengthwise fold. For the front, cut in a curved line on the lower piece from *f* toward *c* to a point slightly more than half way, as shown.

If a pointed sleeve is desired, measure up 3½ inches from *b* on the sleeve line and then cut in a diagonal line from *a* to the 3½-inch point.

Cutting Out the Neck.—Now, to cut the neck, as in Fig. 4, open out the blouse on the crosswise fold and turn it so that the folded edge is toward you and the back or short part of the blouse, comes to your left. Measure up on the crosswise crease 4½ inches and mark with a pin, as at *a*. Measure 1 inch on the back fold from the crosswise crease and mark with a pin, as at *b*. Measure to the right from the crosswise crease 4½ inches and mark with a pin, as at *c*.

Cut the front-neck curve by cutting from *c* to *a* and the back curve by cutting from *b* to *a*.

Utilizing the Under-Arm Sections.—When the blouse is cut, it should appear as in Fig. 5, which shows also the sections cut out at the under arms. Use one of these sections for cutting 1½-inch bias binding for finishing the neck, the bottom of the sleeves, and the pockets, and the other for 6- by 9-inch pockets, as shown. Shape the flaps of the pockets if the sleeves have been shaped, but if they are straight, cut the pockets the same size but with a straight turn-over at the top.

Put a pin 4½ inches up on crease.

Put a pin 1 inch to left. Put a pin 4½ inches to right.

Lengthwise fold

Fig. 4

If pockets are not desired and the sleeve is cut straight, the under-arm pieces may be used as straight cuffs to extend the length of the sleeve.

Proportioning the Skirt

You now cut the belt and skirt from the larger piece of material, as in Fig. 6. For the belt, measure 2½ inches from one selvage edge and cut a strip the full length of the material, cutting on a lengthwise thread. Measure the skirt length from the cut edge down toward the selvage. The material that remains may be used for a hem.

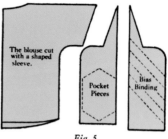

The blouse cut with a shaped sleeve.

Pocket Pieces

Bias Binding

Fig. 5

The skirt material should be wide enough to provide for the hip measure plus 6 inches for ease and 20 inches for plaits, each of the two large plaits taking up 8 inches, or 16 inches for both, and each of the four small plaits 1 inch, or 4 inches in all. Thus, if your hip measure is 40 inches, you will need 40 + 26, or 66 inches.

The dress is now cut and ready for stitching.

Making the Blouse

Binding the Neck.—The first step is to seam the binding strips to make a center-stitched binding for the neck. To do this, join two or three bias pieces, as in Fig. 7, by placing the lengthwise edges together, stitching in a ¼-inch seam, and pressing open with the fingers. Sometimes two and sometimes three pieces are required for the neck, as the length of the pieces depends on the width of the material and the size of the hip measure. Piecings are not objectionable in the bindings, providing the seams are carefully stitched, surplus edges trimmed away, and the seam then pressed open.

Bias bindings may be bought prepared ready for use. Some of these are lovely and many are made in organdie, lawn, and silk, so they are suitable for all fabrics. Hercules braid, also, is desirable as a finish for silk or wool tailored dresses. In using Hercules braid, fold it lengthwise and press it carefully before starting to apply it as binding. The crosswise ends will join more neatly if a row of machine stitching is placed across each one to avoid stretching.

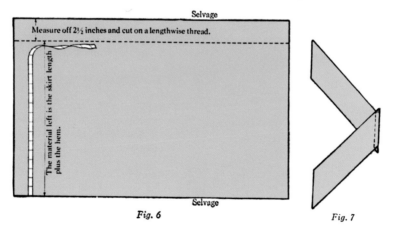

Selvage

Measure off 2½ inches and cut on a lengthwise thread.

The material left is the skirt length plus the hem.

Selvage

Fig. 6

Fig. 7

Stitch the bias edges of the binding together, as at *b*, before making the turn.

Fig. 8

Fig. 9

Place the right side of the binding to the wrong side of the neck and stitch in a ¼-inch seam, as shown at *a*, Fig. 8. Begin stitching at one shoulder and stitch across the back of the neck and around toward the front. Do this easily and without stretching either the neck or the binding. Stitch all the way around and join the binding in a bias seam where it meets, as at *b*, that is, on a lengthwise thread, just as the other joinings were made.

Crease the binding on the under side up from the stitching line *a*, Fig. 9. Then turn the free edge of the binding over ⅜ inch, as at *b*, drawing the edge up smooth and even and creasing as straight as possible. Turn the creased edge *b* down well over the stitching line *a*, and stitch through the center, as at *c*. Begin the stitching at the shoulder and proceed around the back as before.

Finishing the Sleeves.—To bind the two sleeves, join three strips of the binding, open the seams, place the right side of the binding to the right side of the sleeve, as at *a*, Fig. 10, and stitch in a ¼-inch seam. Turn the binding to the wrong side and make a center-stitched binding. Turn back in cuff effect, as shown at *b*.

When the material is attractive on the wrong side, a turn-over center-stitched binding, as in Fig. 11, may be made from the sleeve itself or as a cuff finish without using a binding piece. To make this, turn ⅜ inch to ½ inch, as at *a*; then make another ½ inch turn, as at *b*. Stitch directly in the center. This will give the same effect as the center-stitched bias binding that is used at the neck.

Finish the neck and sleeves, then stitch the under-arm seams.

Fig. 10

When this finish is applied, as in a cuff or a cascade, turn the edges in at the corner in square effect and stitch, as at *c*.

Completing the Blouse.—With the sleeve finish completed, sew the under-arm seams, right sides together, for a French seam. Turn and complete the seams. At the bottom of the sleeves, turn and stitch back in the stitching line just made about 1 inch to secure the cuff edge and to stay the thread ends.

Right Side of Material

Fig. 11

After the skirt length is measured, the remainder of the material may be turned to the right side in a cuff hem.

Fig. 13

To stay the hem, take a back-stitch every 6 or 7 stitches.

Fig. 12

Making the Skirt

Putting in the Hem.—Now, with the blouse stitched, proceed to make the skirt, which has just one seam. Before seaming it, decide on the hem finish. A plain hem may be turned and machine-stitched in or it may be slip-stitched, as in Fig. 12. Before slip-stitching a hem, first turn the top of the hem edge down ¼ inch, as at *a*, and stitch by machine. This gives a firm edge that will aid in keeping a straight line and also protect the slip-stitches. To slip-stitch easily, hold the skirt side next to you, as at *b*, having the fingers on the hem side. Take up as little material with each stitch as possible. To avoid pulling or puckering the hemming-stitches, hold the hem secure and take a back-stitch every six or seven stitches, as at *c*.

A simple yet smart and attractive finish and an excellent substitute for a hand hem is the cuff hem shown in Fig. 13. This should be put in before the skirt seam is stitched.

To make a cuff hem, turn the hem portion to the right side, as at *a*, creasing on a lengthwise thread. Turn the edge over ⅜ inch, as at *b*, and turn the fold ½ inch, as at *c*. Press down and stitch directly in the center.

Seaming the Skirt.—If a cuff hem is used, prepare to French seam the skirt, as in Fig. 14. Pin the bottom *a* and top *b* of the hem ends together so that they will be perfectly even and cannot slip during the stitching.

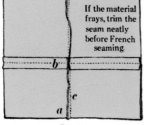

If the material frays, trim the seam neatly before French seaming.

Fig. 14

Contrary to the regular rule, begin the stitching of the skirt at the bottom. Stay the end of the seam by beginning 1 inch from the bottom, as at *c*, stitching to the bottom, and then turning and stitching the full length of the seam. Turn wrong side out and complete the French seam, remembering to stay each end.

If you desire, the hem may be omitted and binding or braid used to finish the bottom of the skirt.

Fig. 15

Joining the Skirt and Blouse

Putting in the Skirt Plaits.—Lay a 4-inch plait on one side of the skirt, having the seam come at the inside of the plait, as shown in Fig. 15. This plait may be laid toward the back or the front, as desired, and should be pressed in straight from top to bottom of the skirt.

About 1½ inches each side of this plait, lay a small plait, about ½ inch deep, as shown, to take up all extra fulness. As both sides are alike, measure half way around the skirt and pin three similar plaits in the opposite side. The edges of each deep plait should come at the under-arm seam of the waist.

If the figure is full across the back in the hips, an inverted plait, with each plait made 2 inches deep and edges turned to meet, is more satisfactory than the deep 4-inch plait.

If soft material, such as crêpe, is used, the sides may be shirred in instead of plaited, as shown in Fig. 16, five or six rows of shirring placed 1 inch apart being desirable. When gathered up, the shirring should take in the allowance of the plaits on each side. A loose, long machine stitch permits a quick, satisfactory shirring. The thread ends of the shirring should be secured with a needle.

Making the Waist-Line Joining.—Next, proceed to pin the skirt to the waist, as shown in Fig. 17, having the edges of the deep plaits, if they are used, meet the under-arm seams. Determine at this time whether you want the plaits to turn to the front or the back. Slip the skirt over the waist with the waist-line edges together, and hold the dress so that you pin the blouse to the skirt, thus preventing its being drawn too tight.

To the notched center front and center back of the waist, pin the centers of the front and the back of the skirt, and place several pins in between these points. By easing in the waist material, the skirt should fit on very well, but if necessary the plaits may be adjusted slightly.

Fig. 16

Fig. 17

Left—Plaid gingham is so decorative in itself as to require only two front tiers of self-material to break its plainness.

Center—Silk crêpe in two harmonizing tones emphasizes its straightness with two tassel-weighted ties of the darker tone.

Left—The softness of the cream-colored chiffon plaited jabot is lovely on the gobelin-blue crêpe de Chine of this dress.

The fulness of the gingham dress just above is confined for the most part in the two deep plaits, one at each side, arranged to turn toward the front. A small amount of fulness is eased on in joining the blouse and skirt. Pin the upper tier to the blouse before joining the skirt. A tiny fold at each end of the tiers, as shown in the sketch, makes them hang correctly. The lower tier is cut slightly longer than the upper one, and its lower edge should be about one-third of the skirt length from the bottom of the skirt.

Ease the fulness of the skirt on very slightly over the hips of the dress above, letting all remaining fulness come in a plait at the left-side back. The one seam of the skirt is arranged to come on the inner edge of this plait. Apply the trimming bands at the center front before finishing the neck, and let the center-stitched binding turn over the ends of the bands. The small sketch shows how these bands are slip-stitched to the blouse part way down to hold them in position. Sleeve piecings are joined with center-stitched binding to look like cuffs.

The skirt of the model above is in wrap-around style, and is finished with a rather deep cuff hem such as is discussed and illustrated on page 15. The overlapping end is hemmed by hand with a 3-inch hem. A narrow machine-stitched hem finishes the other end. Ease in the skirt fulness slightly over the hips. Apply the plaited frill with center-stitched binding before finishing the neck line, so that the end may be finished in the neck binding as illustrated in the little sketch. The plaited sleeve trimming extends over the top only.

Left—Navy-blue novelty crêpe makes this attractive dress with front and back aprons, lace collar and cuffs, and ribbon tie.

Center—Fine gingham in brown, gold, and white is the ideal choice for the model with modish front fulness. Brown velvet ribbon forms the left-side trimming.

Right—A lace-edged jabot of self-material extends the entire length of this model of novelty voile with red and yellow embroidered figures.

In making the dress above, pin the two tiers, the edges of which are finished with center-stitched binding, to the blouse, folding in the blouse fulness a wee bit over the hips in front, as shown in the small sketch. The edges of the two tiers meet at the under-arm seam. Two deep plaits, one at each side, take care of most of the skirt fulness. A slight amount is eased in all the way around. The side plaits turn toward the front, their outer edges coming even with the under-arm seam. The belt is made double and is tacked over the joining of waist and skirt.

The gingham frock above very modishly confines all of its fulness to the front where it is held by machine shirring, as shown in the little sketch. The one seam of the skirt comes at the left side in line with the under-arm seam of the blouse. The plaids must be matched in two places—in the back where the blouse and skirt join and in the left-side seam of the skirt. Do not cut any material away from the skirt in matching the latter seam; rather add 1 or 2 inches to bring the figure in the right location, if necessary. Tack the velvet ribbon on the shoulder and under the bias belt.

In joining the blouse and skirt of the dress above, ease in the fulness slightly all around, but particularly over the hips. The skirt seam is arranged to come at the center-front where it is covered by the full-length jabot. All edges of the jabot are finished with center-stitched binding. Across the top and down the left side, the lace is slipped under the edge and caught in the same stitching that holds the binding. Turn and crease the binding on the opposite side, but pin it to the dress before stitching so that only the single stitching is needed.

Left—Printed crêpe de Chine is chosen for the dress with twin tiers that form soft cascades over the hips. The binding is of Georgette crêpe or ribbon.

Center—A material with some body, such as linen or Canton crêpe, develops this model most successfully.

Right—Buttercup-yellow printed crêpe or voile is trimmed with finely plaited sections of Georgette or plain voile, caught in an unusual way under the belt. Plaiting finishes the sleeves.

The cascade apron front of the model above is cut in two sections, both perfectly straight. Two sides and half of the third are finished with center-stitched binding. The fourth edge is bound with harmonizing Georgette, as shown in the small sketch. Pin the unfinished edges of the aprons to the blouse, having the Georgette-bound edges meet at the center front. In joining the blouse and skirt, ease in the fulness and have the skirt seam come as a continuation of the left under-arm seam. The neck line is cut square in front and round in the back. Like the sleeves, it is finished with center-stitched binding.

A very modish way of disposing of skirt fulness is to lay it in an inverted plait at the center front, as in the model in the center above. The one seam of the skirt comes in one of the inside folds of the plait, as shown in the little sketch at the right. It is necessary to ease in a little skirt fulness all the way around to have the skirt hang correctly and to keep the plait from swinging open at the bottom. The straight, short tunic must be shaped slightly at the waist line in order to hang correctly. The ends are slightly deeper from top to bottom than is the center back. No fulness is evident in the tunic.

The skirt seam of the model at the right comes in the inside fold of a deep plait at the right-side front. This plait is hidden by the finely plaited drape or panel. Cut off a 10-inch length of Georgette and have it hemstitched through the center from selvage to selvage. This, when cut on the hemstitching, provides the picot-edged frills for the sleeves. Hemstitch lengthwise through the center of a piece of Georgette long enough for the plaited drapes. Cut on the hemstitching and use one half for the blouse drape and the other for the skirt drape, picoting the ends of these drapes.

Fig. 18

Fold 5-inch piece
of belt like this

Fold 2-inch piece of belt around

Fig 20

For a slender figure, place the pocket 4½ inches down from the waist line and on the edge of the plait.

For larger figures, place it 2 inches in from the plait.

Fig. 19

When the waist and skirt are pinned together, stitch all the way around by machine, using a $\frac{3}{8}$-inch seam and overlapping the stitching for a couple of inches. Then overcast the raw edges, as in Fig. 18, taking up a number of stitches at one time in order to do the work quickly.

For materials that are too heavy to French seam, overcast the other seams by means of this group overcasting, as shown.

Making the Pocket and Belt

If pockets are used, finish the upper edge with a center-stitched binding, as in Fig. 19. Turn the lap over to the right side and pin the pockets accurately in position, turning in the edges $\frac{3}{8}$ inch. Begin $\frac{1}{2}$ inch from the top, stitch to the top, and then back to stay the top edge securely.

Make the belt as explained for the One-Piece Dress. Then, to make a tailored bow for the belt, cut off a piece of the belt material 5 inches long. Fold the ends to meet in the center, as shown in Fig. 20, and tack down. Cut off another piece 2 inches long, fold this around the first piece at the center, as shown, and tack down.

Sew the tailored bow to one end of the finished belt. If the belt will slip over your shoulders, sew both ends of the belt to the bow. If not, put snap fasteners on the belt. Secure the bow just in front of the left-side seam.

The Dress on the Cover

For the evening dress on the cover you will need one full length of 40-inch material for the back, and for the front a length equal to the distance from the shoulder to the top of the lower tier.

Plan the depth of the tiers, bearing in mind that the lace adds 2 or 2½ inches to the depth of each, and that 1¼ to 1½ inches must be allowed for finishing and joining each tier. Remove a 13-inch strip from one side of the material. Since the depth of the tiers is probably less than 13 inches, remove any excess width and use it for the narrow scarf attached to the left shoulder. Cut each tier 40 inches wide and finish the lower edge with center-stitched binding and lace.

Follow the instruction on pages 8 and 9 in cutting the dress. Before joining the under-arm seams, attach the lower tier to the bottom of the short front length, and the second above this, using a plain seam or a small heading. Make a cuff hem in the back as wide as the lace on the tiers. Join all seams.

*Home of the
Woman's Institute*

Learn at Home to Make
All Your Own Clothes

THE "One Hour Dress" was created by Mary Brooks Picken, Director of Instruction of the Woman's Institute of Domestic Arts and Sciences. This great school at Scranton, Pa., is the largest school of dressmaking and designing in the world and teaches exclusively by the home study method.

Mrs. Picken created the "One Hour Dress" especially to demonstrate how easily you can make attractive clothes when you have proper instructions. The directions in this book are just an example of the amazingly simple methods used in the Woman's Institute new Course in Dressmaking and Designing.

This new Course presents an entirely new way of learning to make your own clothes, based on the Institute's successful experience in teaching more than 200,000 women and girls. It is a new method by which you start at once to make actual garments, a new plan so fascinating that you will want to spend every spare moment in planning and making the many pretty clothes you have always wanted, but never felt you could afford to buy.

By this new method, you, too, can now quickly learn in spare time, in your own home, to make all your own clothes, or you can prepare to take up Dressmaking as a business—secure a good-paying position or open a shop of your own.

It costs you nothing to find out all about the Woman's Institute and what it can do for you. Just send a letter, post card, or the convenient card enclosed and you will receive, without obligation, the full story of this great school and just how it can help you. Please state whether most interested in home or professional dressmaking.

Woman's Institute
Dept. 410, Scranton, Pa.

264WI—15080

CPSIA information can be obtained
at www.ICGtesting.com
Printed in the USA
413010LV00001BA/1